My First Bible

Mercè Segarra

Illustrated by Armelle Modéré

Good Books

God created the world step by step.
The first step was to create light
in the daytime and darkness at night.
Secondly, He created the sky,
the seas, the mountains, the trees
and the flowers.

Creation

Thirdly, He created
the sun, the moon
and the stars.
Fourthly, He created
the animals.
And in the fifth
and final step,
He created humans
to love the earth.

Adam and Eve

The first man and the first woman
that God created were called
Adam and Eve and they lived
in a marvelous place:
The Garden of Eden.
God told them they could eat
the fruit from any tree, except
the one in the very middle
of the garden.

But an evil serpent convinced them to eat it. When God discovered that they had tasted the forbidden fruit, He became angry and banished them from the garden.

Building the Ark

The earth became ever more populated. Many people were not good and they forgot about God, except for Noah.

God asked him to build a large boat, an ark,
because He was going to flood the earth, but
Noah and his family could save themselves.

Flooding the Earth

God asked Noah to board a pair of each kind of animal onto the ark, as well as himself and his family.

Then it rained for forty days and forty nights and everything was flooded. But Noah, his family and the animals were safe, because they were in the ark.
When it finally stopped raining, they left the ark.
And as a promise that He would never harm the earth again, God made a rainbow.

Abraham and Sarah were a married childless couple of advanced age. One day, God told Abraham to go and live in another place, which He would indicate to him.

Abraham and Sarah

Abraham obeyed and together with his wife took their sheep and goats and they began the journey to an unknown destination.

Isaac

One night, Abraham heard God tell him:
"This is the earth, which I give to you
and your children."
"But I have no children," replied Abraham sadly.
"And I can't have any now. I'm too old."
 "Look at the sky, Abraham. Can you see the stars?"
Abraham nodded.
"And can you count them?" God asked him.
"No. Nobody can," replied Abraham.

Then God said to him:
"Listen to me carefully, Abraham. You will have
a son and you'll have grandchildren."
God kept his promise. One year later, Sarah
had a son called Isaac.

Esau and Jacob

Isaac and Rebecca had twin sons, called Esau and Jacob, who were very different from one another. When Jacob grew up, he decided to live in his uncle's house very far away.

14

One night, while traveling, he slept resting his head upon a stone and he had a dream: He saw a long ladder that reached up to the heavens and angels going up and down. God was at the top and He said to him: "Jacob, I will never abandon you. And also, I will give you lots of children and land." From that day onwards, Jacob was never afraid again.

Joseph

Jacob had twelve sons. One was called Joseph, and Jacob loved him so much that he gave him a very beautiful tunic.

His brothers were jealous of him.
So, one day, while the flocks were
grazing, they robbed him of his tunic
and sold him to some merchants
who took him far away, to Egypt.

Joseph in Egypt

While Joseph was in Egypt, God protected him. Also, He gave him the ability to interpret the meanings of dreams.

One day, the King of Egypt (the Pharaoh) summoned him, because he wanted to know the meaning of two dreams he had had. They meant that Egypt would have seven years in a row of good harvests, followed by seven years of poverty and famine. Joseph advised him to store up the food during the seven years of abundance to feed the people when the years of poverty arrived.

When the period of famine arrived, Jacob
sent all his children, apart from Benjamin,
the youngest, to buy food in Egypt.

Joseph's Brothers

Joseph saw them and without revealing to them who he was, he asked them to go and get their younger brother. When they were all together, he told them who he was and forgave them for what they had done to him in the past. In the end, they all went back to Egypt together.

Israelites in Egypt

After several years, there was another Pharaoh in Egypt who hadn't met Joseph.

This Pharaoh was afraid, because
many Israelites had come to Egypt
in search of food and many of
them were powerful. To stop them
from rebelling against him, he
decided to enslave them and also
ordered for all the Israelite male
children to be thrown into the river.

Moses

An Israelite mother had a son and she didn't want to throw him into the river. So she made a straw basket, placed her son inside and put it in the river.

The basket floated away until it got stuck
in some reeds. The Pharaoh's daughter
found it and decided to keep the child
and bring him up as if he were her son.
She named him Moses, which means
"drawn from the water."

Bush in Flames

When Moses grew up, he discovered that he was an Israelite and not an Egyptian. When he saw how his people lived, he decided to escape from the palace and go to the desert.

When he arrived, he saw a burning bush and went closer.
Suddenly, he heard God say to him from the bush:
"Go back to Egypt and ask the Pharaoh to free the Israelites."
Moses obeyed, but the Pharaoh didn't want to free them.

Leaving Egypt

Since the Pharaoh didn't want to
free the Israelites, God decided
to punish the Egyptians by sending
them plagues. When the Pharaoh
saw this, he was frightened and let
the Israelites leave. Then Moses
guided his people to the Promised
Land, or the Land of Canaan.
This departure from Egypt
is known as the Exodus.

When the Israelites left Egypt, the Pharaoh's army followed them. When they reached the Red Sea, the Israelites didn't know how they were going to cross it.

Splitting the Sea

But God sent a very strong wind to help them and the next day, they found a path between two walls of water. So, they were able to cross the sea and reach the desert.

God Gave Bread

Although the Egyptians had fled, the Israelites wandered through the desert exhausted from thirst and hunger.

Moses asked for God's help and He
promised them that bread would fall
from the sky like rain. And so it was:
It rained bread called manna, which
tasted like wafers made with honey.

The Israelites reached Mount Sinai.
One day it was covered with mist
and there was a great storm.

The Ten Commandments

God called Moses and He gave him two
stone tablets with the laws the people
of Israel should follow. These laws were
called the Ten Commandments.

The Ark

God ordered His people to build an ark, a kind of chest, to hold the tablets with the Commandments.

While they traveled through the
desert, the Israelite soldiers
watched over it and when they
stopped, they placed it in a tent
decorated with tapestries. For
them, it was like a temple, where
they prayed and worshipped God.

The Horns of Jericho

After many years, Moses died and God chose
Joshua as Israel's new guide. His mission was
to lead his people to Canaan.
The first city they reached was Jericho. They
were unable to enter, because it was surrounded
by very high walls. Then God told Joshua to
walk around the city blowing horns. They did
so for six days and on the seventh, the walls fell
down and they were able to enter the city.

Samuel

The Israelites conquered those lands, but they were not always good people. God gave Israel some guides (the judges and prophets), who helped the Israelites to follow the path of good.

The last of these guides was Samuel, who ruled for many years. When he grew old, he chose his children to govern, but the people were tired and asked him to choose a king for the people.

Saul

Samuel chose Saul as
the first king of Israel.
Saul was very strong and
defeated many enemies.

But the people stole things,
kept them and didn't share
them with anybody. God
was not pleased with this
and He asked Samuel
to choose another king.

Samuel chose the young shepherd David as the new king. David was very brave and he fought Goliath, who was a giant from the enemy army, feared by everybody.

David and Goliath

David beat the giant and was a good king. He made Jerusalem the capital of his kingdom and God helped him.

King Solomon

When David died, his son Solomon became the new king of Israel. He asked God for wisdom, because he wanted to rule well.

As he was not asking for material goods,
God was pleased and gave him many riches.
To thank Him, Solomon built a temple
in Jerusalem dedicated to God.

Daniel and the Lions

Daniel was a great prophet. He lived in the court of the king of Babylon, where he was a counselor. In Babylon, the people worshipped false gods and there was a law that punished anybody who failed to worship them.

As Daniel was loyal to God, he was punished.
They threw him into a pit of lions. But he was not
afraid, because he trusted that God would protect
him from the lions. And they did not harm him.
Thus the Babylonians realized that Daniel's God
was the true God.

Jonah and the Whale

God asked Jonah the prophet to go to Nineveh and ask the people to be good. Jonah didn't want to go and he boarded a ship to escape.

While he was on the ship, there was a great storm and Jonah realized that it was his fault for not listening to God's orders. So, he asked for the sailors on the ship to throw him into the sea. When he fell into the water, he was swallowed by a great whale. He asked God for forgiveness and God forgave him.

The Annunciation

One day, an angel appeared before Mary, who lived in Nazareth, and told her that she would have a son and that he would be called Jesus.

Mary excitedly went to see her cousin Elizabeth, who was also pregnant. Elizabeth was the mother of the last prophet, John the Baptist, who prepared the hearts of the people for the arrival of Jesus.

The Birth

Mary married Joseph, who was a carpenter. They both went to Bethlehem.

After a long journey, they were very tired and looked for a place to stay, but they couldn't find anywhere, because there were a lot of people. Luckily, a man let them sleep in his stable. Jesus was born that night.

Good News

The night when Jesus was born, some shepherds were sleeping in the countryside near Bethlehem. Suddenly, the sky lit up and an angel appeared before them and told them that a baby had been born in Bethlehem and that he was the savior. The shepherds hurried to go and see him.

The Kings from the East

Far away from Bethlehem,
in the East, there lived
three very wise men.

One night, a very bright star appeared before them and they thought that it was a sign from God, so they loaded their camels and followed the star, which led them to the stable where Jesus was born. They worshipped him and gave him gold, incense and myrrh.

Jesus and his family lived in Nazareth.
When Jesus was twelve years old,
his parents took him to Jerusalem to
celebrate Passover.

Jesus in the temple

When the festivities were over, everybody went home. Mary and Joseph thought that Jesus was among the people who were returning. Then they realized that he was not with them, so they went back to Jerusalem to look for him. They found him in the temple, speaking with the teachers, who were teaching people things about God. Jesus asked them about God and they were impressed by how he spoke.

The Baptism

Jesus's cousin, John the Baptist, lived in a desert. One day, while he was in the River Jordan, encouraging people to be good and baptizing them, Jesus appeared and he asked John to baptize him.

While John baptized him,
God spoke, referring to Jesus:
"This is my son."
That's how everybody discovered
that Jesus was the son of God.

The Disciples of Jesus

Jesus knew that the time had come to travel the land and teach that God loved everybody and to ask people to love each other.

He needed men to help him to spread
these messages. So, he chose
twelve helpers, most of whom were
fishermen, who he called disciples.

The Wedding at Cana

Jesus and his disciples were invited
to a wedding. While Mary was helping
with the wedding, the wine ran out.

Then Mary asked her son to do something, because she felt sorry for the bridegroom and his family. Jesus performed his first miracle: He converted six jugs of water into very good wine. Henceforth, his disciples believed and trusted him more.

Jesus Heals the Sick

Jesus traveled throughout
the world for three years.

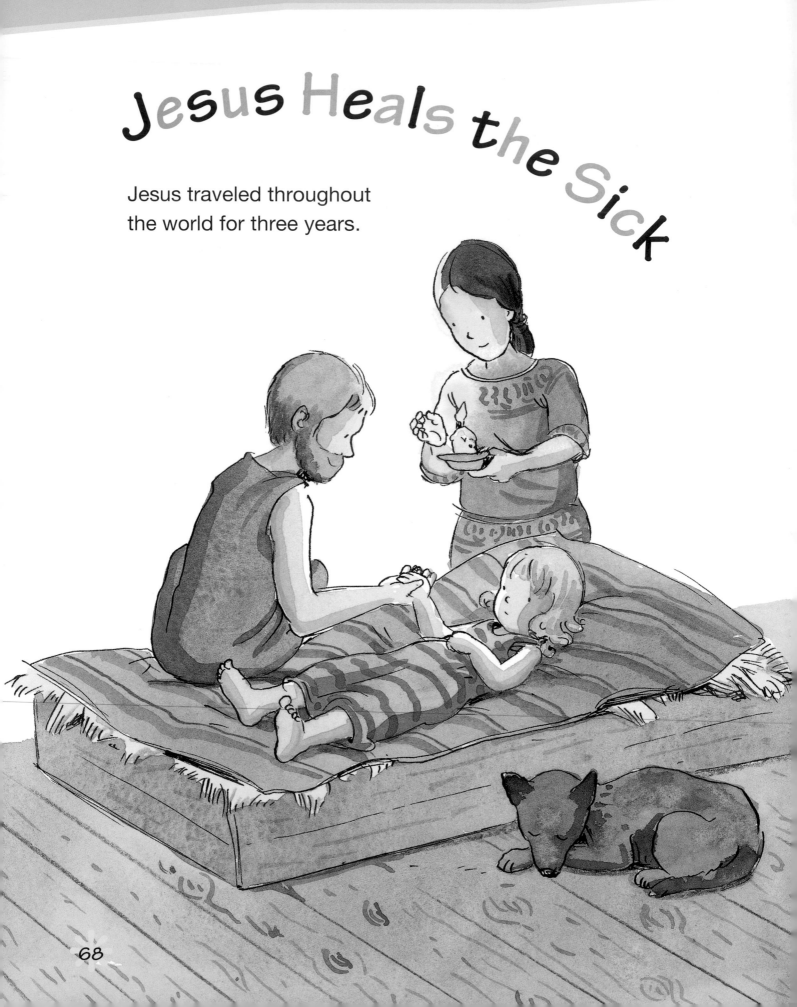

Every time he reached a city, he
was greeted with great enthusiasm,
because he had the power to heal
the sick, just by touching them.

Jesus was also known for telling beautiful stories about the love of God: the parables.

The Parables

Each of these parables had a message
for the people to be good and understand
that God loved and forgave everybody.

Parable of the Two Sons

A man had two sons and he asked the elder to go and work in the vineyard owned by the family.

He replied that he didn't want to go, but later,
after thinking about it, he regretted his answer and
decided to go and work. The father did the same with
the younger son, who quickly replied that he would
go to work straight away, but in the end, he didn't go.
Which of the two sons followed his father's will?

Parable of the Two Houses

Jesus said: "He who listens to my words and puts them into practice is like the sensible man who builds his house by digging the foundations in the rock.

The rain fell, the wind blew, torrents crashed against the house, but it was not knocked down, because it had good foundations. However, he who listens to my words and fails to put them into practice is like the foolish man who builds his house on the sand. The rain fell, the wind blew, the torrents crashed against the house and it collapsed, because it did not have good foundations."

Parable of the Grain of Mustard

Jesus also said to his friends: "What I want from you is for you to be a grain of mustard.

When it is sown, the mustard is one of the smallest seeds on the earth, but when the plant is born and grown, it becomes the largest of all the plants in the garden. Its branches grow very long and the birds of heaven take refuge in its shade."

A shepherd had 100 sheep and he lost one.
He left the other 99 and went to look for the
one that had gotten lost until he found it.

Parable of the Lost Sheep

Then he returned home very pleased
and gathered together all his friends
to tell them the good news.

One day, some parents took
their children to Jesus, so
that he could bless them.
But the disciples told them
that Jesus was very busy.

Jesus and the Children

Jesus saw that the parents
and children were very sad
and he got angry with the
disciples. Then he blessed
each of the children.

To Jerusalem

One spring, Jesus and his disciples went to Jerusalem to celebrate Passover.

Jesus rode on a donkey and the people
greeted him with branches of olive and palms.
He was very moved to see everybody adoring
him and he entered the city like a king.

The Betrayal of Judas

The high priests thought that
Jesus had power over the people
and they wanted to kill him.

Judas, one of Jesus's disciples, did not love him and he didn't understand him either. So, he told the priests where they could find him, in exchange for thirty pieces of silver.

The Last Supper

Jesus knew that he was going to die
soon and he wanted to celebrate
the last Passover supper with his
disciples. Although he was sad, he
tried to hide it and encouraged them
to love one another as he had loved
them. During the meal, they drank
and ate bread. Jesus told them that
whenever they gathered together for
Passover, they should remember him.

The Olive Grove

After the supper, Jesus went to pray in an orchard at the Mount of Olives.

Some of the disciples followed him.
Suddenly, Judas appeared with the high
priests' soldiers and they arrested Jesus
and took him to Pontius Pilate, the governor.

The Crucifixion of Jesus

Pontius Pilate asked Jesus whether he was the son of God and he said yes.

Pilate wanted to free Jesus, because he though that he had done nothing wrong, but the high priests wanted to kill him and Pilate listened to them. Finally, Jesus died after being crucified on a hill outside the city.

The Resurrection

Jesus' friends buried him in a cave and sealed the entrance with a great rock.

Three days later, three women went and saw that the stone had been moved. Then an angel appeared before them and told them that Jesus had been resurrected and they went running to the disciples.

The Ascension

After coming back to life, Jesus appeared
to his friends on several occasions.

One day, he explained to them that he was about to go up to heaven with God, but he promised them that he would send them the Spirit of God, who would help them to be strong and to tell his story and spread his message of salvation to the people. Several days later, a holy fire came down to rest on the shoulders of his disciples. It was the power that Jesus had transmitted to them to help them spread what he had taught them throughout the world.

10 9 8 7 6 5 4 3 2 1

Library of Congress Control Number: 2019950485

Text by Mercè Segarra
Illustrations by Armelle Modéré
Design and layout by Gemser Publications, S.L.

Print ISBN: 978-1-68099-491-9
Ebook ISBN: 978-1-68099-492-6

Printed in China